A. PHILIP
RANDOLPH

and the
Labor Movement

by Robert Cwiklik

GATEWAY CIVIL RIGHTS
THE MILLBROOK PRESS
BROOKFIELD, CONNECTICUT

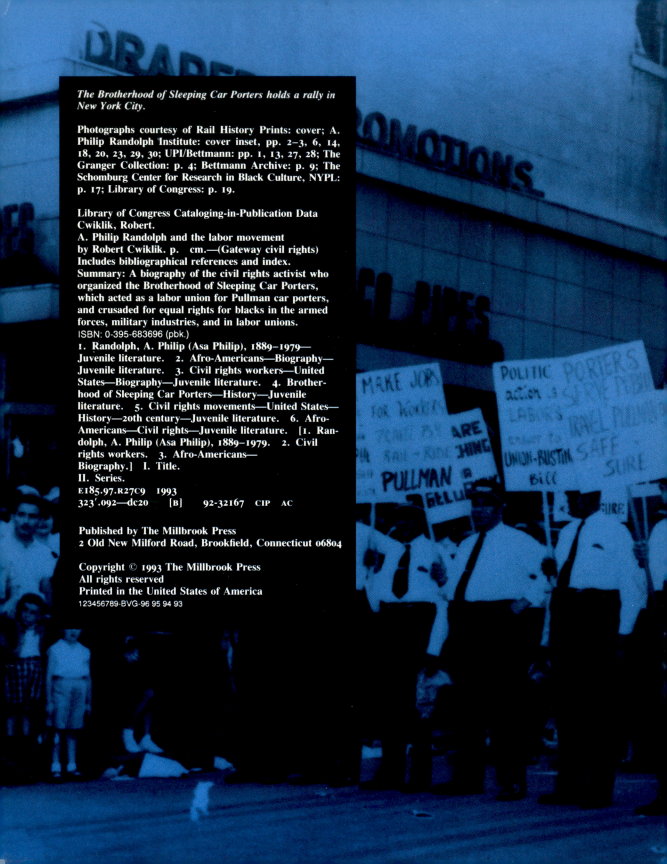

The Brotherhood of Sleeping Car Porters holds a rally in New York City.

Photographs courtesy of Rail History Prints: cover; A. Philip Randolph Institute: cover inset, pp. 2–3, 6, 14, 18, 20, 23, 29, 30; UPI/Bettmann: pp. 1, 13, 27, 28; The Granger Collection: p. 4; Bettmann Archive: p. 9; The Schomburg Center for Research in Black Culture, NYPL: p. 17; Library of Congress: p. 19.

Library of Congress Cataloging-in-Publication Data
Cwiklik, Robert.
A. Philip Randolph and the labor movement
by Robert Cwiklik. p.   cm.—(Gateway civil rights)
Includes bibliographical references and index.
Summary: A biography of the civil rights activist who organized the Brotherhood of Sleeping Car Porters, which acted as a labor union for Pullman car porters, and crusaded for equal rights for blacks in the armed forces, military industries, and in labor unions.
ISBN: 0-395-683696 (pbk.)
1. Randolph, A. Philip (Asa Philip), 1889–1979—Juvenile literature. 2. Afro-Americans—Biography—Juvenile literature. 3. Civil rights workers—United States—Biography—Juvenile literature. 4. Brotherhood of Sleeping Car Porters—History—Juvenile literature. 5. Civil rights movements—United States—History—20th century—Juvenile literature. 6. Afro-Americans—Civil rights—Juvenile literature. [1. Randolph, A. Philip (Asa Philip), 1889–1979. 2. Civil rights workers. 3. Afro-Americans—Biography.] I. Title.
II. Series.
E185.97.R27C9   1993
323′.092—dc20   [B]   92-32167   CIP   AC

Published by The Millbrook Press
2 Old New Milford Road, Brookfield, Connecticut 06804

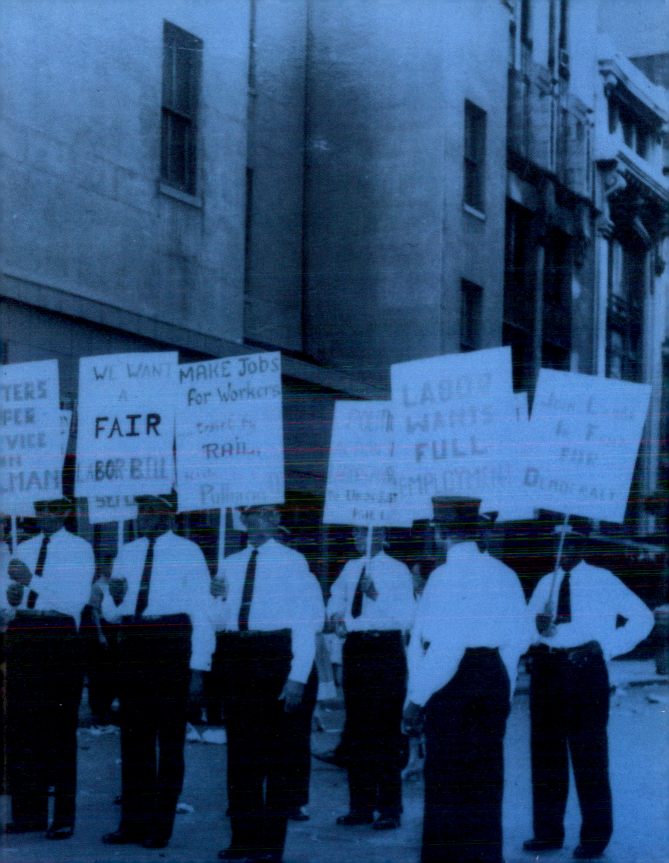

On the evening of August 25, 1925, a large crowd of mostly black men gathered in a meeting hall in New York City. The men worked as sleeping-car porters for the Pullman Company. Their jobs were very hard. They were forced to work one hundred hours per week—twice as long as most workers—making beds, polishing shoes, cleaning clothes, and serving meals. They were paid an average of fifteen dollars per week, much less than other workers on the railroad. And they had to buy their uniforms and meals out of their slim salaries. Most white men were too proud to take such low jobs. But black men had to take whatever work they could find.

Most porters believed that the Pullman Company treated them unfairly. The porters' only chance to improve their lot was to organize themselves into a union. Then porters all across the country could refuse to work unless their demands for better pay and shorter hours were met.

That night at the meeting hall, the porters in the audience waited nervously to hear a speech about forming a union. The Pullman Company fired any workers suspected of organizing unions. It was known that spies from the Pullman Company were also in the audience. The porters were afraid they could lose their jobs, but they also knew something had to be done.

Passengers on Pullman sleeping cars were well served by porters and waiters, who were poorly paid and overworked.

The leaders of the Brotherhood at a meeting in Harlem.
A. Philip Randolph stands fifth from the right.

The main speaker for the night was a young, handsome black man named A. Philip Randolph. When he walked proudly onto the big stage and began to speak, his clear, commanding voice made the porters forget their fears for a while. Somehow his words changed how they felt about themselves. He made them believe they deserved better treatment and should fight to get it. He made them feel powerful.

The day after the meeting, two hundred porters joined the new union, the Brotherhood of Sleeping Car Porters. Their work was just beginning, though. Sleeping-car porters across the nation had to be convinced to join them. Money, talent, and hard work were needed to do the job. Luckily, A. Philip Randolph was a talented speaker and organizer. He raised money from friends and soon left on a trip around the country to win new members for the Brotherhood.

Over the years, Randolph and his followers would change the face of labor relations in the United States. Randolph not only battled for porters, he also fought for the rights of blacks in the armed forces, in military industries, and in labor unions. He inspired many young people to pick up where he left off in the fight for social justice for black Americans. To these crusaders, A. Philip Randolph was "the father of the civil rights movement."

We'll Walk

Asa Philip Randolph was born on April 15, 1889, in Crescent City, Florida. The Civil War had been over for almost twenty-five years. But many of the problems of that earlier time had still not been solved. Although blacks were no longer enslaved, they were still mistreated in America, especially in the South.

For a short time after the war, the United States government tried to do many things to improve the lives of black people. This period was called the Reconstruction Era. The Fourteenth and Fifteenth amendments to the United States Constitution guaranteed the rights of citizenship to black people—including the right to vote. Blacks were elected to legislatures in Southern states, where they helped make laws. Black children went to the same schools as white children.

But the Reconstruction Era ended in 1877 when Northern troops were pulled out of the Southern states. Southerners were bitter about having so many new laws forced on them by Washington. Black people in the South felt the brunt of their anger. So-called Jim Crow laws were passed, which barred blacks from riding in railroad cars used by whites, or going to white schools or white hospitals. Many public places began to sport signs reading WHITES ONLY. Blacks were kept from voting or holding public office. Those who didn't ''remember their place'' risked death at the hands of white lynch mobs.

Things were a little better for blacks in Florida, where young Asa lived with his parents and older brother. A short time after Asa was born, his father, James William Randolph, moved the family from Crescent City to Jacksonville, where he was a preacher in an African Methodist Episcopal Church. In Jacksonville, blacks still used public facilities with whites, went to

*By the end of the nineteenth century, Jim Crow
laws were spreading through the South. Blacks
and whites used separate public facilities.*

the library, and rode with them in buses. Some blacks even
held public office. But blacks in Jacksonville were still much
poorer than whites and had fewer chances to move up in life.

Asa's father didn't make much money as a preacher.
Sometimes the poor blacks in his congregation could only af-
ford to give him sacks of potatoes for pay. Still, the family
was rich in many ways. James Randolph was a strong man,

who had been lucky enough to get a good education. He had grown to love books and learning, and he stocked his home library with fine writing. Often he would take down a book and read to his sons. His clear, powerful voice, trained by years of preaching, made the words come to life in their minds.

Asa's mother, Elizabeth, was a beautiful woman who was also very able. She raised chickens in the yard and other food for the family table in her garden—collard greens, tomatoes, peas, and strawberries. She also brought in extra money as a seamstress.

Asa learned many things from his parents and from his older brother James, a quiet boy who liked to study and share what he learned. Both boys did well in school. From time to time, a jealous classmate would pick on one of them, and Asa or James would get into a fight. But Elizabeth didn't get angry. She wanted her sons to learn to defend themselves.

Elizabeth was wise to teach her sons to grow brave and strong. The lives of black people were getting harder. Jim Crow laws had spread to Florida, and the U.S. Supreme Court upheld them. In the case of *Plessy* v. *Ferguson,* the court said it was legal for states to have separate facilities for blacks and whites. It was legal for blacks to be barred from white schools, lunch counters, and parks. These things may have been legal, but to blacks and some whites they didn't seem right.

Asa's parents taught their sons to fight back. When a black prisoner faced lynching by whites, James grabbed his rifle and stood guard around the jailhouse with a group of armed black men. Elizabeth held a shotgun in her lap to protect the children from the mob. Asa and James would never forget their parents' bravery. Nor would they forget their father's reaction when Jim Crow laws came to Jacksonville. When blacks were forced to ride in the back of the bus and give up their seats if a white person asked them to, James said that his family would not ride buses anymore. He said that, from then on, the Randolphs would walk.

The Man of the Hour

At the age of fourteen, Asa enrolled in the Cookman Institute, a high school and junior college run by Methodists, where his brother was also a student. Cookman was the only school in the area where blacks could go for a higher education. Asa did very well there. He blossomed into a very good-looking young man, and his teachers and classmates noticed his special talents. Asa organized reading groups to share the love of books he had learned at his father's knee. He read from his favorites, such as the Bible or Shakespeare, in a dramatic style that had his fellow students hanging on his every word.

Asa developed his talents. He practiced good posture, throwing his shoulders back and holding his head high and proud. He pronounced words over and over to himself until he got them just right. He and his friends formed a theater group and put on plays at community gatherings. He also studied hard and read widely. One book was a favorite, *The Souls of Black Folk,* by the famous African-American author W. E. B. Du Bois. It held a message of hope for blacks and told them to fight for full equality.

African Americans did not all think alike about how to deal with racism in the United States. Many agreed with Booker T. Washington, who said blacks should accept racism for the time being and focus on bettering themselves through hard work. Washington was very popular with whites. But Du Bois said that blacks should openly oppose racism. In 1907, Asa graduated from high school at the head of his class. He was chosen to give the graduation speech. His topic was Du Bois, whom he called "the man of the hour."

After graduation, Asa took a job with an insurance company. But he knew his talents could carry him further. Asa's parents had always hoped that he and James would follow in their father's footsteps and become ministers. Asa was good at organizing people and getting things done. He was also an excellent public speaker, with a voice that was truly a gift, clear

W. E. B. DU BOIS

W.E.B. Du Bois was one of the most influential African-American leaders of the early twentieth century. He was born in Great Barrington, Massachusetts, in 1868, and he became the first black sociologist in the United States. He wrote the first studies of the way black people live in America.

Du Bois was also a very important protest leader. He criticized the ideas of Booker T. Washington, who advised blacks to accept, for the moment, white racism. Du Bois believed that the lives of African Americans

W.E.B. Du Bois.
His writings moved
Randolph very deeply.

could be improved only through protest. In his most famous book, *The Souls of Black Folk,* he said that Washington's ideas would only keep blacks in chains.

As he grew older, Du Bois grew more radical. In 1961 he joined the Communist party, gave up his U.S. citizenship, and moved to Ghana, a nation in West Africa. He died there in 1963 at the age of ninety-five.

and strong like the chiming of a church bell. Asa might have made a fine minister. But he had other ideas, such as becoming a famous actor.

But it was hard for Asa to fulfill his ambitions in Jacksonville, where blacks were not given good jobs. He quit the insurance company and worked for a time on the railroad laying track and shoveling coal. For a young man of his ability, there had to be something better.

A friend told Asa about a job in the kitchen of a boat bound for New York City. Asa had spent a summer there during high school and had found the place exciting. In the South, blacks were barred from college. But there were colleges in New York that admitted blacks. Asa Philip Randolph took the job on the boat and was soon steaming north to a new life.

Troublemaker

Soon Randolph settled in Harlem, the black section of New York City, and enrolled in City College, which was located there. The year was 1911, and blacks from all over the South were coming to Harlem, including many gifted artists, writers, and musicians.

A young Asa, dressed to the nines.

Randolph was thrilled by the richness of Harlem life. He also became absorbed in his schoolwork. His main subjects were history and economics. He was especially drawn to the ideas of the economic philosopher Karl Marx. Marx said that the owners of factories and businesses—capitalists—had too much power and that workers should unite to demand higher wages and better working conditions. Then one day, they would revolt against the owners. All the factories would be in the hands of the people, and everyone would share the wealth.

Randolph grew fascinated with socialism—the name given to Marx's ideas—and also began to study labor unions. If workers banned together into unions, they could go on strike, refusing to work unless they got higher pay and better treatment. Randolph saw hope for black people in socialism and labor unions. But when he made speeches about such things to church groups in Harlem, his audiences were cold. They believed that the Lord would take care of them, so they didn't see the need for direct action on their part.

Randolph attended classes at night, and worked at odd jobs by day to support himself. He had not yet decided what his life's work would be. He was still interested in acting and performed in several plays. But the political life of Harlem also attracted him, the speakers who drew huge crowds on street corners with their talk about the need for blacks to rise up and demand their rights.

For a time, Randolph worked as a janitor at a local utility company. He tried to convince other black workers there to unite and demand better treatment. But they didn't want to make waves. Randolph soon quit in disgust. His next job was as a waiter on a steamboat, where he tried to organize the kitchen help to demand that their filthy, rat-infested living quarters be cleaned up. Instead, the owner fired him from the ship for being a "troublemaker."

Marchers in New York City protest an anti-black riot in St. Louis. When Randolph moved to Harlem, blacks were demanding equal rights in a louder voice than ever before.

Then Randolph was asked to join a theater company. His dream of being a professional actor seemed to be coming true. But his parents were against it. In their eyes, acting wasn't a serious job. Sadly, he turned the offer down. But he still had his passion for politics. He now devoted himself fully to improving the lives of black people. He didn't worry about getting ahead in a career. He later said that the most important thing in his life at this time was "creating unrest" among African Americans.

"The Most Dangerous Negroes in America"

Randolph threw himself into work with the Independent Political Council (IPC), a group that taught poor people about socialism and unions. He also met Lucille Campbell Green, a stylish young woman. She, too, was a socialist, and she admired Randolph very much. The two were soon married.

Lucille introduced Randolph to a man who would become a close friend, Chandler Owen, a student at Columbia University. He was a sharp-dressing, witty man who loved to talk politics. Owen and Randolph hit it off quickly and were soon working together, organizing and making speeches for the IPC. Randolph became president, and Owen became executive secretary. Despite their lofty titles, the work didn't pay much. But Lucille made a good living as a hairdresser and gladly supported them.

Lucille Randolph

Chandler Owen was Randolph's good friend. They worked hard to talk black workers into creating their own unions.

Randolph and Owen were soon drawing huge crowds to their open-air speeches in Harlem. They spoke about what concerned blacks most—racial injustice. The United States was now setting aside segregated, or separate, facilities for whites and blacks in government buildings. Lynching and other violent crimes against blacks were on the rise. There were even anti-black riots.

Randolph and Owen believed that if blacks joined unions, they could fight back. But whites would not allow blacks into their unions. The two men decided to form a union for black workers. They began by organizing some six hundred black elevator operators. But the effort failed. The operators, fearing they would lose their jobs, refused to go on strike.

A union of restaurant workers offered Randolph and Owen office space if they would put out a newspaper for them. The two agreed, and the *Hotel Messenger* was born. They filled the paper with news about the labor movement. But when they wrote about restaurant workers who were cheating their fellow workers, the two were fired for embarrassing the union.

But they would not be silenced. In 1917 they started a magazine, the *Messenger*. Its pages exposed wrongs suffered by the poor and African Americans. During World War I, black men were shamed even when they joined the army to fight for their country. They were put in all-black squads to do servants' work.

The *Messenger* called on poor whites and blacks to unite and fight for the rights of workers everywhere. Blacks were urged not to join the army, not to fight for justice overseas until they had won it at home.

The government saw the *Messenger* as a threat. U.S. agents ransacked its offices. Randolph and Owen were arrested for telling people not to join the army. But at their trial, the judge set them free. He didn't believe these young blacks could have written such intelligent articles. The judge thought the writing must have been done by whites who had set up Randolph and Owen to take the blame.

The *Messenger* and its authors were becoming famous. Randolph and Owen went right on making speeches, sharing their beliefs with audiences all over the country. Washington watched them closely. Agents at the Department of Justice called them ''the most dangerous Negroes in America.''

The Brotherhood

The early 1920s was a time of trouble for Randolph. Lucille's business was suffering. Many of her clients were afraid to have their hair done by the wife of a ''dangerous radical.'' To make matters worse, Randolph's father died, and his friend Owen moved to Chicago, unhappy with the way white socialists treated blacks. Randolph also quit the socialists. But he did not give up his ideals.

In June of 1925, Randolph got an offer that changed his life. Ashley Totten, a porter for the Pullman Company, asked him to help Pullman porters form a labor union. Randolph was stunned. He had never had much luck forming unions and wasn't sure he was right for the job. But when the porters pleaded, he agreed to help.

After Randolph spoke at the wildly successful meeting on August 25, 1925, he went on a cross-country trip to win members for the new union, the Brotherhood of Sleeping Car Porters. At first some porters did not trust this neatly dressed, well-spoken, big-city black man. But Randolph usually won them over with his speeches. If he could not, then the fiery words of Ashley Totten, who traveled with him, often did the job.

Randolph traveled far and wide, spreading the union message. He raised money for train fare by passing a hat for donations at rallies. He was so poor that when his mother died, he didn't have enough money to travel to her funeral. But he kept on. By the end of 1926 the Brotherhood had chapters across the country.

At first the Pullman Company ignored the union, believing it would never be a serious threat. Then the company fought back hard. It put out a newspaper filled with lies about Randolph and the union. Randolph was said to be planning to steal $72,000 from the porters' union money to run off to Russia.

Some porters believed the lies and began to doubt the union and its leader. But Randolph convinced most to stay the course. The struggle grew harder for him in 1928 when his brother James died. The two had been very close, and Randolph was greatly saddened. But instead of slowing down to mourn his loss, he drove himself on to build the union.

Randolph speaks at a meeting for the newly formed Brotherhood of Sleeping Car Porters. He traveled all over the country inviting porters to join.

Randolph had hoped that the Pullman Company would one day meet with the union to work out a new deal for the porters. When that didn't happen, the workers bravely voted to go out on strike. Randolph was warned by a white labor leader that the Brotherhood would be beaten by the powerful company. He let his doubts sway him and called off the strike.

The company fought back anyway. It fired every porter it believed had voted to strike. Porters grew afraid of being linked to the Brotherhood. Its membership fell from seven thousand to around seven hundred. After just one blast of the company's hot breath, the union seemed to be melting away.

Many porters believed Randolph had caused this disaster by calling off the strike. They stopped buying the *Messenger*. The Brotherhood, many believed, was dead.

"Let the Negro Masses Speak"

While others lost hope for the union, Randolph fought on. After years of struggle, he managed to get the Brotherhood into the American Federation of Labor (AFL), which for years had barred blacks.

But in 1929 the Great Depression hit, and millions all over the nation lost their jobs. Since work was so hard to get, porters were even more afraid to join the Brotherhood, especially since it seemed so weak.

The tide turned when Franklin D. Roosevelt became president in 1933. His support for unions made workers bolder. But the Pullman Company didn't budge. It fired many porters and created its own union. Then it said that any new porters that wanted a job had to join the company union. Of course, the company's own pet union was not going to stand up to the company's bosses for the workers.

When Randolph complained, the government decided to hold an election to see which union the porters wanted, the company's or the Brotherhood. In a way, the porters were voting on A. Philip Randolph's life's work. It was no contest. The Brotherhood won, 8,316 votes to 1,422. Randolph proudly called this vote the first victory for black workers over a giant corporation.

Now the Pullman Company had to sit down and deal with the Brotherhood. The union won many things for the porters, including a big pay increase, and a cut in hours from 400 a month to 240. And A. Philip Randolph won praise across the nation for his bold, progressive leadership.

But Randolph was not done fighting. In 1941 he organized a march on Washington, D.C., to demand that companies making military supplies begin to hire blacks. It soon looked like

100,000 people would march. "Let the Negro masses speak," said Randolph. To make him call off the march, Roosevelt wrote new rules granting the demands. The great W. E. B. Du Bois, Randolph's lifelong hero, called his victory "astonishing." In June 1942 more than 20,000 blacks cheered Randolph at a rally in New York's Madison Square Garden. It was "the biggest demonstration of Negroes in the history of the world," he said. And he had more face-offs with presidents. In 1948 he and others pressured President Harry S. Truman to put an end to Jim Crow laws in the military.

Randolph continued to be active in the union movement. In 1955, when the AFL joined the CIO to form one massive union, Randolph was named a vice president. He was thrilled by the great victories of the civil rights movement in the fifties and sixties. Younger leaders hailed him as "the father of the civil rights movement."

Even at the age of seventy-four, Randolph still played a role in the movement. He helped to organize the great March on Washington in 1963, when over a quarter of a million people went to the capital to press for new civil rights laws. Sadly, Lucille had died a few months before, but Randolph went and delivered the first speech of the day. Then he introduced Dr. Martin Luther King, Jr., who made his memorable "I have a dream" speech.

Labor and civil rights leaders met with President John F. Kennedy in 1963 during the March on Washington.

After the Civil Rights Act passed in 1964, Randolph worked to ensure voting rights for black Americans. He also spoke out against the Vietnam War. But his influence waned in the mid-to-late sixties, when race riots rocked U.S. cities. Randolph spoke out against the violence and was criticized by younger black leaders, who said he was out of step with the times.

Randolph retired from the Brotherhood in 1968. He died in 1979, at the age of ninety.

A. Philip Randolph's life was studded with victories. Over the years, he won many honors. In 1942, the National Association for the Advancement of Colored People (NAACP) awarded him its Spingarn Medal. In 1964, President Lyndon Johnson gave him the nation's highest civilian honor, the Medal of Freedom. During that same year, the A. Philip Randolph Institute was set up in Washington, D.C., to make sure that his life's work would go on.

President Lyndon Johnson gives Randolph the Presidential Medal of Freedom in honor of his lifelong effort to improve people's lives.

IMPORTANT EVENTS IN THE LIFE OF A. PHILIP RANDOLPH

1889	Randolph is born on April 15 in Crescent City, Florida.
1911	Randolph moves to Harlem in New York City, New York, and marries Lucille Campbell Green.
1917	A. Philip Randolph and Chandler Owen publish a magazine called the *Messenger*.
1925	Randolph becomes an active leader in the Brotherhood of Sleeping Car Porters.
1935	The Brotherhood is voted the official union of the Pullman Company.
1941	Randolph threatens a march on Washington, D.C., to protest the lack of black employees in defense industries. President Roosevelt meets his demands.
1942	Randolph receives the Spingarn Medal from the NAACP.
1955	Randolph becomes a vice president of the AFL-CIO.
1964	President Lyndon B. Johnson awards Randolph the Medal of Freedom, and the A. Philip Randolph Institute is founded.
1979	Randolph dies on May 16.

FIND OUT MORE ABOUT
A. PHILIP RANDOLPH AND HIS TIMES

Books: *The Civil Rights Movement in America from 1865 to the Present* by Patricia and Fredrick McKissack (Chicago: Childrens Press, 1987).

The Labor Movement in the United States by John J. Flagler (New York: Lerner Publishing, 1990).

W. E. B. Du Bois and Racial Relations by Seamus Cavan (Brookfield, Connecticut: The Millbrook Press, 1993).

Places: A. Philip Randolph Institute
1444 I Street N.W.
Suite 300
Washington, D.C.
Phone: (202) 289-2774

A. Philip Randolph, ''the father of the civil rights movement,'' and Bayard Rustin, civil rights leader and director of the A. Philip Randolph Institute.

INDEX

Page numbers in *italics* refer to illustrations.

Brotherhood of Sleeping Car Porters, 7, 21-22, *23*, 24-25

Du Bois, W.E.B., 12, 13, *13*, 26

Harlem, 15-16
Hotel Messenger, 19

Jim Crow laws, 8, *9*, 10, 11, 26
Johnson, Lyndon B., 28, *28*

Kennedy, John F., *27*
King, Martin Luther, Jr., 26

Labor unions, 5-7, *6*, 16, 19, 21-22, *23*, 24-25
Lynching, 8, 19

Madison Square Garden rally (1942), 26
March on Washington (1963), 26
Medal of Freedom, 28, *28*
Messenger, 20-21, 24

National Association for the Advancement of Colored People (NAACP), 28

Owen, Chandler, 18-21, *19*

Plessy v. *Ferguson* (1896), 10
Pullman Company, *4*, 5, 21, 22, 24, 25

Randolph, A. Philip, 6, *14, 27, 30*
    birth of, 7
    death of, 28
    education of, 10, 11, 15-16
    employment of, 15-17
    family of, 8-11
    in Harlem, 15-16
    honors award, 28
    labor unions and, 5-7, *6*, 16, 19, 21-22, *23*, 24-25
    marriage of, 18
    Messenger and, 20-21
    as public speaker, 12, 15
    socialism and, 16
Randolph, Elizabeth, 10, 11, 17, 22
Randolph, James, 10-12, 22
Randolph, James William, 8-11, 17, 21
Randolph, Lucille Campbell Green, 18, 21, 26
Reconstruction Era, 8
Roosevelt, Franklin D., 25, 26
Ruskin, Bayard, *30*

Socialism, 16
Souls of Black Folk, The (Du Bois), 12, 13
Spingarn Medal, 28

Totten, Ashley, 21, 22
Truman, Harry S., 26

Voting rights, 8, 27

Washington, Booker T., 12, 13